## SHORT WALKS
**MADE EASY**

# GREATER MANCHESTER

Ordnance Survey

# Contents

| | | |
|---|---|---|
| Getting outside in Greater Manchester | | 6 |
| We smile more when we're outside | | 8 |
| Respecting the countryside | | 10 |
| Using this guide | | 11 |
| **Walk 1** | Manchester to Salford Quays | **14** |
| **Walk 2** | Clifton Country Park | **20** |
| Photos | Scenes from the walks | 26 |
| **Walk 3** | Wigan Pier and The Flashes | **28** |
| **Walk 4** | Jumbles Country Park and Turton Tower | **34** |
| Photos | Wildlife interest | 40 |
| **Walk 5** | Irwell Vale to Ramsbottom | **42** |
| **Walk 6** | Hollingworth Lake | **48** |
| **Walk 7** | Dove Stone Reservoir | **54** |
| Photos | Cafés and pubs | 60 |
| **Walk 8** | Etherow Country Park | **62** |
| **Walk 9** | Sale Water Park | **68** |
| **Walk 10** | Dunham Massey | **74** |
| Credits | | 80 |

| | |
|---|---|
| Map symbols | Front cover flap |
| Accessibility and what to take | Back cover flap |
| Walk locations | Inside front cover |
| Your next adventure? | Inside back cover |

2  Short Walks Made Easy

---

## Walk 1

### MANCHESTER TO SALFORD QUAYS

**Distance**
4.5 miles / 7.2 km

**Time**
2½ hours

**Start** Manchester Victoria Station

**Finish** Media City UK

**Parking** M4 4DY
Euro Car Parks – Miller Street car park

**Cafés/pubs**
Manchester; Salford Quays

### The perfect introduction to the great city of Manchester

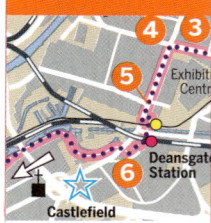

Page 14

## Walk 2

### CLIFTON COUNTRY PARK

**Distance**
2 miles / 3.1 km

**Time**
1¼ hours  *CATCH A BUS*

**Start/Finish**
Clifton Country Park

**Parking** M27 6NG
Clifton Country Park car park

**Cafés/pubs**
Café at the visitor centre

**Explore a beautiful, green oasis on a former colliery site**

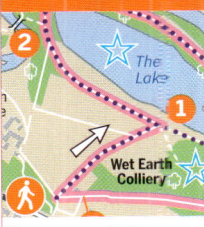

Page 20

## Walk 3

### WIGAN PIER AND THE FLASHES

**Distance**
4.6 miles / 7.4 km

**Time**
2¾ hours  *GO BY TRAIN / CATCH A BUS*

**Start/Finish**
Wigan

**Parking** WN3 4EH
Trenchfield Mill car park

**Cafés/pubs**
Wigan; Ince-in-Makerfield

**A canal corridor and green spaces with a rural feel from Wigan**

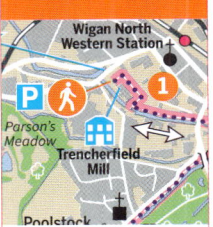

Page 28

## Walk 4

### JUMBLES COUNTRY PARK AND TURTON TOWER

**Distance**
3.75 miles / 6 km

**Time**
2¼ hours  *GO BY TRAIN / CATCH A BUS*

**Start/Finish**
Jumbles Country Park

**Parking** BL2 4JS
Waterfold car park

**Cafés/pubs**
Cafés at the visitor centre and Turton Tower; Chapeltown

**Splendid Pennine views, lake, woods, meadows and a 700-year-old tower**

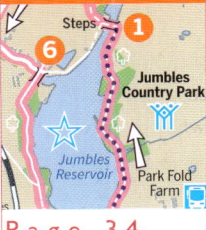

Page 34

Contents  3

## Walk 5

### IRWELL VALE TO RAMSBOTTOM

**Distance**
2.7 miles/4.3km

**Time**
1½ hours

**Start** Irwell Vale
**Finish** Ramsbottom

**Parking** BL0 0QG
Irwell Vale Station car park

**Cafés/pubs**
Cafés at Irwell Vale and Stubbins; Ramsbottom

**Linear old railway walk in the Irwell valley, returning by steam train**

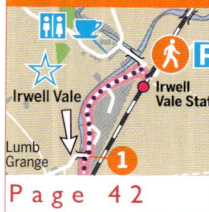

Page 42

## Walk 6

### HOLLINGWORTH LAKE

**Distance**
2.3 miles/3.7km

**Time**
1½ hours

**Start/Finish**
Smithy Bridge

**Parking** OL15 0DQ
Hollingworth Lake Bank car park

**Cafés/pubs**
Lakeside Café; Pavilion Café; The Wine Press; The Beach

**Attractive lakeside circuit, Pennine views and waterside cafés**

Page 48

## Walk 7

### DOVE STONE RESERVOIR

**Distance**
2.8 miles/4.5km

**Time**
1¾ hours

**Start/Finish**
Dove Stone Reservoir

**Parking** OL3 7NE
Dove Stone Reservoir car park

**Cafés/pubs**
Picnic benches; Greenfield

**Scenic reservoir circuit in Manchester's corner of the Peak District**

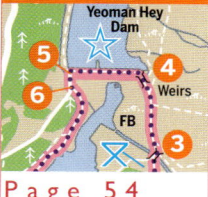

Page 54

4 Short Walks Made Easy

## Walk 8

### ETHEROW COUNTRY PARK

**Distance**
2.6 miles/4.2km

**Time**
1½ hours  *CATCH A BUS*

**Start/Finish**
Compstall

**Parking** SK6 5JD
Etherow Country Park car park

**Cafés/pubs**
Country park and Potting Shed cafés; Andrew Arms

**Lush, wooded valley; old mill village history and a patron of industry**

Page 62

## Walk 9

### SALE WATER PARK

**Distance**
2.6 miles/4.2km

**Time**
1½ hours  *TAKE A TRAM*

**Start/Finish**
Sale Water Park

**Parking** M33 2LX
Jackson's Boat car park

**Cafés/pubs**
Tree Tops Café; Jackson's Boat (pub)

**Mersey stroll; Broad Ees Dole Nature Reserve; lake-based activities**

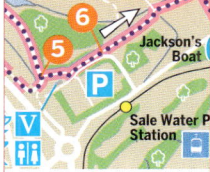

Page 68

## Walk 10

### DUNHAM MASSEY

**Distance**
5.2 miles/8.3km

**Time**
3 hours  *CATCH A BUS*

**Start/Finish**
Oldfield Brow, Altrincham

**Parking** WA14 5RF
Trans Pennine Trail car park

**Cafés/pubs**
NT café; four pubs en route

**Lovely old railway path; Dunham Massey parkland; rural canal towpath**

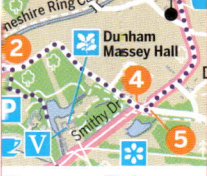

Page 74

# GETTING OUTSIDE IN GREATER MANCHESTER

❝❞
Routes at Dove Stone Reservoir and Etherow Country Park enable you to experience Manchester's corner of the Peak District

OS Champion
Samantha Meekin

Smithy Drive, Dunham Massey

# A very warm welcome to the new Short Walks Made Easy guide to Greater Manchester — what a fantastic selection of leisurely walks we have for you!

The great city of Manchester, its metropolitan surroundings and urban fringes provide the setting for the ten splendid short walks, which embrace the city centre, the green spaces and blue corridors of Greater Manchester, and the scenic countryside within easy reach of the city. Beginning amid the grand architecture in the historic heart of Manchester, the opening walk is a station-to-station route to the modern steel and glass buildings of Media City in rejuvenated Salford Quays. Excellent Transport for Greater Manchester connections are used to whisk walkers by tram, train and bus to locations from Wigan to Stockport and Ramsbottom to Altrincham.

In Wigan, old miners' paths and railway trackbeds lead you through the waterscapes of The Flashes on a walk with an unexpectedly rural feel. Pennine views are the objective on the Turton Tower ramble from Jumbles Country Park. Explore the Irwell valley on foot then return from Ramsbottom via steam train, or enjoy the lakeside cafés at Hollingworth in a lovely shore circuit. Routes at Dove Stone Reservoir and Etherow Country Park enable you to experience Manchester's corner of the Peak District. Four rural pubs and a National Trust café dot the route through the landscaped deer park of Dunham Massey, and you can follow winding nature reserve trails around the oasis of Sale Water Park.

**Samantha Meekin, OS Champion**

**WE SMILE MORE WHEN WE'RE OUTSIDE**

The former Great Northern Railway Company's Goods Warehouse

Whether it's a short walk during our lunch break or a full day's outdoor adventure, we know that a good dose of fresh air is just the tonic we all need.

At Ordnance Survey (OS), we're passionate about helping more people to get outside more often. It sits at the heart of everything we do, and through our products and services, we aim to help you lead an active outdoor lifestyle, so that you can live longer, stay younger and enjoy life more.

We firmly believe the outdoors is for everyone, and we want to help you find the very best Great Britain has to offer. We are blessed with an island that is beautiful and unique, with a rich and varied landscape. There are coastal paths to meander along, woodlands to explore, countryside to roam, and cities to uncover. Our trusted source of inspirational content is bursting with ideas for places to go, things to do and easy beginner's guides on how to get started.

It can be daunting when you're new to something, so we want to bring you the know-how from the people who live and breathe the outdoors. To help guide us, our team of awe-inspiring OS Champions share their favourite places to visit, hints and tips for outdoor adventures, as well as tried and tested accessible, family- and wheelchair-friendly routes. We hope that you will feel inspired to spend more time outside and reap the physical and mental health benefits that the outdoors has to offer. With our handy guides, paper and digital mapping, and exciting new apps, we can be with you every step of the way.

**To find out more visit os.uk/getoutside**

# RESPECTING
# THE COUNTRYSIDE

You can't beat getting outside in the British countryside, but it's vital that we leave no trace when we're enjoying the great outdoors.

Let's make sure that generations to come can enjoy the countryside just as we do.

Leave no trace

Keep dogs under control; bin and bag waste

Do not light fires; only BBQ at official sites

Leave gates as you find them

Keep to footpaths and open access land

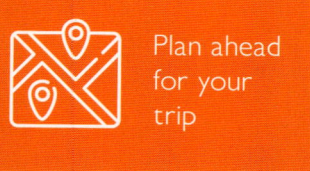
Plan ahead for your trip

For more details please visit gov.uk/countryside-code

# USING THIS GUIDE

## Easy-to-follow Greater Manchester walks for all

### Before setting off

**Check the walk information panel to plan your outing**

- Consider using **Public transport** where flagged. If driving, note the satnav postcode for the car park under **Parking**
- The suggested **Time** is based on a gentle pace
- Note the availability of **Cafés**, tearooms and pubs, and **Toilets**

**Terrain and hilliness**

- **Terrain** indicates the nature of the route surface
- Any rises and falls are noted under **Hilliness**

**Walking with your dog?**

- This panel states where **Dogs** must be on a lead and how many stiles there are – in case you need to lift your dog

- Keep dogs on leads where there are livestock and between April and August in forest and on grassland where there are ground-nesting birds

### A perfectly pocket-sized walking guide

- Handily sized for ease of use on each walk
- When not being read, it fits nicely into a pocket...

- ...so between points, put this book in the pocket of your coat, trousers or day sack and enjoy your stroll in glorious countryside – we've made it pocket-sized for a reason!

### Flexibility of route presentation to suit all readers

- **Not comfortable map reading?** Then use the simple-to-follow route profile and accompanying route description and pictures

- **Happy to map read?** New-look walk mapping makes it easier for you to focus on the route and the points of interest along the way

- **Read the insightful Did you know?, Local legend, Stories behind the walk** and **Nature notes** to help you make the most of your day out and to enjoy all that each walk has to offer

## OS information about the walk

- Many of the features and symbols shown are taken from Ordnance Survey's celebrated **Explorer** mapping, designed to help people across Great Britain enjoy leisure time spent outside

- National Grid reference for the start point
- Explorer sheet map covering the route

**OS information**
🚶 SJ 840989
Explorer 277

## The easy-to-use walk map

- **Large-scale** mapping for ultra-clear route finding

- **Numbered points** at key turns along the route that tie in with the route instructions and respective points marked on the profile

- **Pictorial symbols** for intuitive map reading, see Map Symbols on the front cover flap

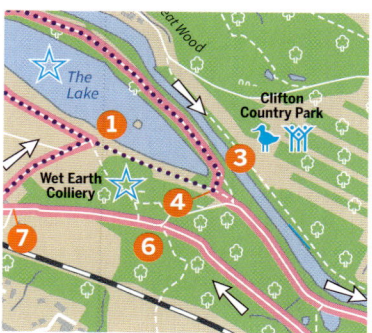

## The simple-to-follow walk profile

- Progress easily along the route using the illustrative profile, it has **numbered points** for key turning points and **graduated distance** markers

- Easy-read **route directions** with turn-by-turn detail

- Reassuring **route photographs** for each numbered point

12  Short Walks Made Easy

## Using QR codes

- Scan each QR code to see the route in Ordnance Survey's OS Maps App.
*NB You may need to download a scanning app if you have an older phone*

- OS Maps will open the route automatically if you have it installed. If not, the route will open in the web version of OS Maps

- Please click **Start Route** button to begin navigating or **Download Route** to store the route for offline use

Greater Manchester 13

# WALK 1

# MANCHESTER TO SALFORD QUAYS

This station-to-station walk is the perfect introduction to the great city of Manchester. You'll pass Chetham's School of Music, the National Football Museum and the 15th-century Cathedral, before seeing the Royal Exchange, St Ann's Square and then the Gothic Town Hall and Central Library, said to be inspired by the Pantheon in Rome. The Bridgewater Canal eases the route through Castlefield to the Manchester Ship Canal, from where you'll reach Media City UK, Salford Quays, with lots of places to eat.

## OS information

SJ 840989
Explorer 277

**Distance**
4.5 miles/7.2km

**Time**
2½ hours

**Start** Manchester Victoria Station
**Finish** Salford Quays, Media City UK

**Parking** M4 4DY
If you can, use Manchester's excellent public transport.
Nearest to: Euro Car Parks, 88A Miller Street (charge)

**Public toilets**
At Manchester Victoria Station and Salford Quays

**Cafés/pubs**
Numerous en route

**Terrain**
Pavement; canal towpath, partly cobbled

14  Short Walks Made Easy

### Hilliness
Mostly flat; towpath ramps to/from the Bridgewater Canal

### Footwear
Year round

### Public transport
National rail services to Manchester Victoria: nationalrail.co.uk; for the return tram service to Manchester Victoria from Media City change at Deansgate Castlefield: tfgm.com

### Accessibility
Accessible throughout, but manual wheelchair users may find the cobbled ramps along the Bridgewater Canal challenging, in which case take the tram from Deansgate/Castlefield, near ❺

### Dogs
Welcome but keep on leads. No stiles

**Did you know?** A post box that was near the centre of the 1996 Provisional IRA bomb explosion survived. It was moved during regeneration work in the city centre but was returned to the site in Corporation Street. It carries a brass plaque recording the explosion. To see it, look/turn left out of Market Street, after ❷.

**Local legend** Some Mancunians believe there is hidden treasure beneath their streets. According to local legend, during the Civil War a local merchant buried his wealth to stop it falling into the hands of plundering soldiers. Over the years many speculators have searched for the bounty but, so far, without success.

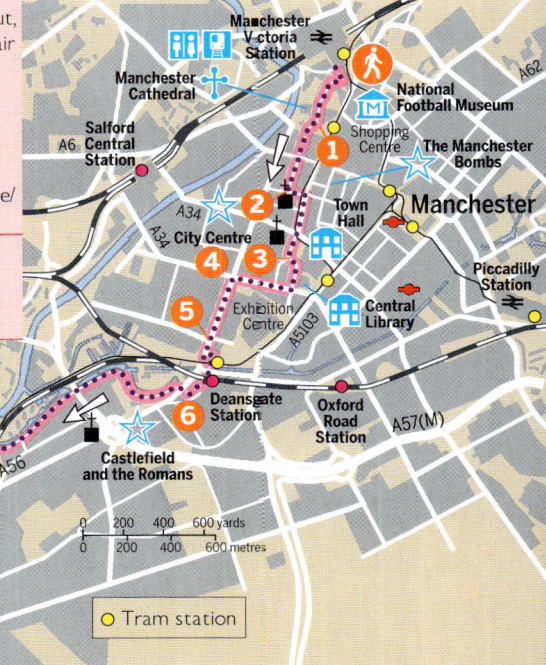

Walk 1 Manchester to Salford Quays

# STORIES BEHIND THE WALK

☆ **City Centre** In 1717, Manchester was a market town with a population of just 10,000; at the turn of the 19th century, it had become the world's largest marketplace for cotton goods and its population had grown exponentially. The city's great wealth was shown for all to see in its ornate, sometimes exotic buildings, like the huge Gothic Town Hall and the Royal Exchange Building, once the hub of the textile industry — its old trading floor was the largest in Europe.

- Leave the station through the archway **left** of the ticket office, cross the road at the pedestrian lights and go **left** along Station Approach.
- Turn first **right** into Cathedral Gardens (National Football Museum); follow the paved road past Chetham's School and Manchester Cathedral to Selfridges.

**1** 
- Keep **ahead** between Selfridges and Harvey Nichols, using either the steps or the ramp to the left, and continue along New Cathedral Street.
- Go **straight on** at the crossroads along Exchange Street to reach St Ann's Square.

### ☆ Castlefield and the Romans

Castlefield is a complex of railways, canals, docks, locks, warehouses and bridges. The area's importance goes back to CE 79 when Gnaeus Julius Agricola built a fort here to protect the Roman road between Chester and York. The fort, *Mamucium* or *Mancunium*, gave its name to the city. Castlefield grew during the Industrial Revolution. The Bridgewater Canal, which links the Manchester Ship Canal to Yorkshire by way of the Rochdale Canal, was the first true canal built in Britain.

**Bridgewater Canal**

The Deansgate

sgate — Deansgate Station — 1½ miles — ⑥ Passage signposted Castlefield Canal Basin — Lift bridge by Greatest Hits Radio — 2 miles

**②** ▶ Turn **left** by the church along St Ann Street then **right** along Cross Street.
▶ Where the tram lines arc left, go **straight on** to Albert Square, walking to the far end and passing Manchester Town Hall.

**③** ▶ Veer **left** at the far end of the square to pass the cylindrical library building.
▶ Then turn **right** by the Midland Hotel onto Peter Street and, in 300 yards, pass the former Great Northern Railway Company's Goods Warehouse to reach a crossroads.

Walk 1 Manchester to Salford Quays

☆ **The Manchester Bombs** The Provisional IRA's bombing of Manchester in 1996 ripped the heart out of the city's shopping centre. The incident initiated a massive regeneration programme. One of the city's oldest buildings, The Old Wellington Inn (1552), was damaged in the blast; it was repaired and relocated with its neighbour, Sinclair's Oyster Bar, to ❶.

☆ **Salford Quays** Home to Media City, a development of luxury apartments, a shopping centre, the Imperial War Museum, the Lowry theatre and the BBC and ITV studios, Salford Quays used to be the site of Salford Docks, which, together with the Pomona Docks, formed Manchester Docks, once the third-busiest port in Britain. The use of containerised cargo started the demise of the docks, which closed in 1982.

| 2½ miles | 3 miles | ❼ |

B r i d g e w a t e r Throstle
        C a n a l         Nest Bridge

❹ ▪ Turn **left** onto Deansgate and follow it past the shops and under the bridge by The Deansgate pub.
▪ Where the main Chester Road curves right, go **straight on** using the pedestrian crossing heading for Deansgate Station.

❺ ▪ Pass the railway station on your left and continue under the railway bridge for 100 yards to a signpost and passageway under a block of flats on the right.

❻ ▪ Turn **right** through the passageway, signed Castlefield Canal Basin.
▪ Stay on the left side of the canal, soon crossing a lift bridge over the dock by Greatest Hits Radio.
▪ Keep following the towpath, canal on your right, for 1½ miles to Throstle Nest Bridge.

# NATURE NOTES

The birds that might be seen along the canals and waterfronts include Canada geese, grey herons, herring and black-headed gulls, mute swans, coots and moorhens. Interesting winter visitors to Salford Quays are tufted duck and pochard.

On the banks of the Bridgewater Canal several species of wildflower grow out of crevices in old walls and cobbled towpaths. These include the tall, pink-flowered, hairy-stemmed great willowherb, and ragwort, whose yellow flowers are poisonous to cattle but are beneficial to insects. Evening primrose thrives on wastegrounds. The tall, yellow, four-petalled plant was introduced to Britain from North America in the 1600s. The oil extracted from it is used in herbal remedies.

Great willowherb

Tufted duck

Media City UK Station

3½ miles — Manchester Ship Canal

4 miles — Second footbridge over the ship canal

BBC building 4½ miles

**7** ▪ Leave the towpath across the bridge and turn **right** down a roadside pavement.
▪ Turn **left** under the overpass to join the towpath of the Manchester Ship Canal.
▪ Go **left** to walk beside the canal for 1 mile to the second footbridge, opposite the BBC building.

**8** ▪ Turn **right** across the bridge to arrive at Salford Quays Media City.
▪ For the tram terminus, go past the BBC studios and angle **right** across a large square.

Walk 1 Manchester to Salford Quays

# WALK 2

# CLIFTON COUNTRY PARK

CATCH A BUS

| OS information | |
|---|---|
| SD 771041 Explorer 277 | |
| **Distance** 2 miles/3.1 km | |
| **Time** 1¼ hours | |
| **Start/Finish** Clifton Country Park | |
| **Parking** M27 6NG Clifton Country Park car park (charge) | |
| **Public toilets** At the visitor centre | |
| **Cafés/pubs** Café at the visitor centre | |
| **Terrain** Good firm tracks around the lake; mostly good dirt and stone track bridleway | |
| **Hilliness** Flat around the lake; elsewhere, very gently undulating | |
| **Footwear** Year round | |

Lying in the Irwell valley south-east of Kearsley, Clifton Country Park covers 120 acres of beautiful forest, meadow and lake, and provides visitors of all abilities with lovely walks. The harshness of the colliery landscape has been enveloped by nature. Well-surfaced tracks encircle the lake and give frequent glimpses of the Wet Earth Colliery's past, including James Brindley's siphon, while revealed in the woodland east of the visitor centre are Gal mine's pit head, the old engine shed and the wheelhouse.

**Did you know?** Clifton Country Park was a favourite haunt of the renowned artist LS Lowry, who painted many scenes from the Irwell valley.

**Local legend** As a young man, James Brindley (1716–1772) gained a reputation for repairing mill machinery, and grew to become a brilliant engineer and prolific canal builder. Among his notable achievements are the Bridgewater Canal (see Walks 1 and 10), the Trent and Mersey, and the Oxford canals. He also devised the hydraulic pump that saved the Wet Earth Colliery (see page 23).

### Public transport
Bus services 8 and 22, between Bolton and Manchester, stop at Clifton Cricket Club on A666, ⅓ mile from ⑥: tfgm.com

### Accessibility
Wheelchair friendly 🚶 to ④, with return by completing a lake circuit; all-terrain pushchair-friendly throughout

### Dogs
Welcome. No stiles

Walk 2 Clifton Country Park

# STORIES BEHIND THE WALK

⭐ **River Irwell**  Rising on Deerplay Moor above Burnley, the River Irwell flows into the Mersey after being canalised to form part of the Manchester Ship Canal. It was once considered to be among England's most polluted rivers, a victim of the Industrial Revolution. In the latter part of the 20th century the river was cleaned up and restocked with fish. At Clifton Country Park these days, you can look down on lively crystal-clear waters.

⭐ **The lake**  The beautiful lake was created after the excavation of stone and gravel used in the construction of the M62 motorway. The grassland and woodland of the marina area are ideal for picnics and leisurely walks. Wooden sculptures are placed around the lakeside paths.

Clifton Park car park

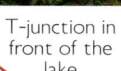
T-junction in front of the lake

The Lake

Fletcher's Canal

Fork

▶ From the far end of the car park, with your back to the visitor centre, go through the gateway on a wide firm track that crosses a large meadow to reach a path T-junction in front of the lake.

❶ ▶ At the junction, turn **left** on another wide track signed Fairy Tale Trail.

▶ Walk parallel to the lake shore for ¼ mile to a fork in the track.

22   Short Walks Made Easy

## ⭐ James Brindley's hydraulic pumping solution

In 1756, famed engineer James Brindley solved the mine's flooding problem with a hydraulic pumping scheme that included building a weir at Ringley Fold. This created a head of water to power a waterwheel, which pumped out the mine before returning the water into the river. In 1790, Matthew Fletcher extended and enlarged Brindley's feeder stream to form a navigable canal – you'll see its channel on the left as you round the northern side of the lake.

## ⭐ Wet Earth Colliery

Clifton Country Park is situated where the Wet Earth Colliery once produced coal for the nation. It lay on the Pendleton Fault, whose geological movement brought the seams of coal much nearer the surface. The first deep mine was sunk here in the 1740s by John Heathcote, aided by mining engineer Matthew Fletcher. The mine suffered flooding from the River Irwell and was temporarily closed, reopening in 1756 after the success of Brindley's hydraulic pump (see left); it remained open until 1928. The Gal Pit was named after Galloway ponies, used for powering a pulley system at the pit. You'll pass a metal sculpture of a pony at the Gal pithead.

## ⭐ The Lake

½ mile

**4** Turn right to return to car park

**3** Gateway

**4** Path junction

**2** ▶ Take the **right** fork and continue round the north shore for ½ mile to a gateway at the far end of the lake.

**3** ▶ Pass through the gateway and turn **right**, walking to the next path junction, **ahead**, in 50 yards.

**Walk 2** Clifton Country Park

# NATURE NOTES

On the lake you may see cormorants, large black birds with long necks. If you're lucky and quick enough, you may also see the electric-blue flash of a diving kingfisher. Teal, gadwall and goldeneye ducks are winter visitors. If you're here in spring, you might be lucky enough to see the fascinating courtship dance of the colourful great crested grebe.

You will almost certainly see Canada geese. Introduced from North America, their population has grown in great numbers throughout Britain – over 50,000 pairs breed here and another 100,000 overwinter.

The riverbanks of the Irwell are infested with giant hogweed, a plant originating from Georgia and Central Asia. Do not touch it as the sap is corrosive and readily burns the skin. Appearing in June, the plant can attain 15 feet in height and has huge spiky leaves and small white flowers clustered on umbrella-like heads.

The grey squirrels at Clifton Park are quite tame – they're obviously used to being fed by the visitors.

Cormorants

**4** ➤ Turn **right** to complete a lake circuit; back at **1**, turn **left** to retrace your steps to the start.

➤ Otherwise, go **left** on a wide bridleway for ⅓ mile, passing two pretty ponds to reach a track junction (red arrow).

**5** ➤ Turn **right** on the track following the red arrow waymarkers.

➤ The track soon turns sharp **right**. Keep **forward** on this track for almost ½ mile to a path junction.

**Top left**: great crested grebe
**Above**: goldeneye
**Top right**: giant hogweed

**Grey squirrel**

Junction with Wet Earth Colliery Trail (keep straight on)

Cycle restrictor gate

**Gal Pit** (pony sculpture)

**Wet Earth Colliery** (right)

2 miles

Clifton Park car park

**6** ▬ At the junction, keep **straight on**, ignoring the side tracks marked with yellow-banded posts (part of the Wet Earth Colliery Trail).
▬ Carry on for 350 yards to a gateway near the visitor centre.

**7** ▬ Approaching the car park, take the **right** fork through the cycle restrictor to complete the walk or, if your pushchair doesn't fit, go through the gate to the **left** and turn **right** past the visitor centre.

**Walk 2** Clifton Country Park

This page (clockwise): Sale Water Park; Compstall Post Office; River Irwell
Opposite (clockwise): Lumb Bridge; railway bridge sign, Strongstry; Dunham Massey mill; Ashway Gap and Dean Rocks

# WALK 3

# WIGAN PIER AND THE FLASHES

This walk around the environs of southern Wigan follows green corridors between the houses and factories of the Wigan Pier Quarter and Ince-in-Makerfield. With help from Wigan Council and the Lancashire Wildlife Trust, nature has returned to cloak the former coalfields. A canal towpath takes you from the pier, through the middle of The Flashes, and old miners' paths and railway trackbeds are used on the return for a pleasant and unexpectedly rural-feeling walk.

## OS information
SD 577051
Explorer 276

**Distance**
4.6 miles/7.4km

**Time**
2¾ hours

**Start/Finish**
Wigan

**Parking** WN3 4EH
Trencherfield Mill car park (charge)

**Public toilets**
Wigan Market, WN1 1PL; Bus Station, WN1 1LR; both railway stations (WN1 1BJ, WN1 1BB)

**Cafés/pubs**
Wigan; Ince-in-Makerfield

**Terrain**
Canal towpath; good, mostly surfaced footpaths

**Hilliness**
Mainly level, with a couple of ramps

**Footwear**
Year round

**Did you know?** Wigan was built on the site of a second-century Roman settlement, Coccium. Much evidence of this has been uncovered and it is thought that a Roman fort stood on the top of The Wiend (WN1 1PF), a strategic position overlooking the River Douglas.

**Local legend** In mining folklore, Red Clogs was a collier who tragically died while operating a coal-washing hopper, which was used to separate soil and rock from the coal. He tried in vain to clear an obstruction in the machine but fell in and was killed by the rotating blades used to crush the coal. The miner's name refers to his blood-stained shoes after the fatal accident. He is said to haunt the whole area and miners were often heard to blame Red Clogs for anything that went wrong.

**Public transport**
National rail services to Wigan North Western Station (West Coast Mainline), 400 yards from 🚶, and Wigan Wallgate Station, 500 yards from 🚶: nationalrail.co.uk; Bee Network bus services to Wigan Bus Station, ½ mile from 🚶 or Clayton Street stop, 100 yards from 🚶: tfgm.com

**Accessibility**
Powered wheelchair and all-terrain pushchair friendly

**Dogs** Welcome. No stiles

**Walk 3** Wigan Pier and The Flashes

# STORIES BEHIND THE WALK

☆ **George Orwell** In 1936, when George Orwell came to Wigan to write *The Road to Wigan Pier*, he noted: 'I remember a winter afternoon in the dreadful environs of Wigan. All round was the lunar landscape of slag-heaps ... in the distance, stretched the 'flashes' — pools of stagnant water that had seeped into the hollows caused by the subsidence of ancient pits ... it seemed a world from which vegetation had been banished; nothing existed except smoke, shale, ice, mud, ashes, and foul water'.

☆ **Wigan Pier** The pier, which became a music hall joke after quips from George Formby Senior, was actually a coal-loading staithe on the canal. Coal from a nearby colliery would have been unloaded here onto barges for transportation around the world. It was demolished in 1929 although recreated in a later renovation of the area. Today, planning has been passed to redevelop the Pier Quarter, turning its warehouses into a housing and leisure complex.

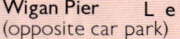

Trencherfield Mill · ½ mile · Canal junction and footbridge · Pearson's Flash (left) 1 mile

Wigan Pier (opposite car park)

Leeds & Liverpool Canal

Trencherfield Mill car park

- Leave by the car park's vehicle entrance on Heritage Way and turn **right**.
- Continue to the Rose Bruford College at the end of the old mill complex.

❶ ▶ Turn **right** along the far side of a lock to reach the canal by the Wigan Dry Dock.
- Turn **left** along the towpath of the Leeds & Liverpool Canal and follow it to a bridge at a canal junction in ⅓ mile.

Short Walks Made Easy

## 🏠 Trencherfield Mill

The gigantic four-storey, red-brick Trencherfield Mill lies across the road from the 'pier' at the start of the walk. The former cotton mill, built in 1907, had a huge four-cylinder engine that powered a large flywheel, and eight billion yards of cloth had been produced by the time the mill closed in 1968. Now apartments, and offices for the Canal and River Trust, the engine is still powered up for visitors on selected dates throughout the year.

## 🐦 The Flashes

'Flashes' refers to the lakes formed by flash flooding after the subsidence of old coal mines in the area early in the 20th century. The demolition of the nearby Westwood Power Station in the 1980s created layers of ash which covered the area around The Flashes, eventually leading to the creation of the reed bed, grassland and woodland habitats seen today. They are now incorporated into The Flashes of Wigan and Leigh National Nature Reserve.

Leeds & Liverpool Canal

Scotsman's Flash (right)   1½ miles   Canal footbridge   2 miles   Archway

lashes

**2** ▪ Go up the ramp, across the bridge and down the shallow-stepped ramp on the far side.

▪ Continue along the towpath of the tree-lined canal for 1¼ miles, passing between two large flashes (lakes) to a footbridge.

**3** ▪ Turn **left** to cross the canal footbridge.

▪ On the other side, go **left** again then fork **right** on an initially stony path.

▪ It soon becomes a good paved path. Ignoring minor side paths, follow it to the nature reserve exit.

Walk 3 Wigan Pier and The Flashes

# NATURE NOTES

Bitterns are brown, thickset herons. They live in the reed beds of The Flashes during winter, and are being encouraged to stay and breed. This rare bird is quite shy although the males have a bellowing boom that they use to attract a mate. Spring sees the arrival of reed warblers, sedge warblers, reed buntings, common terns and water rails.

Although they're seen in numbers here, the willow tits are an endangered species elsewhere in Britain. They're slightly larger than a blue tit but without the bright colours. This mid-brown bird has a black cap with white cheeks.

The ashes that covered the area have created great conditions for many wildflowers. Orchids such as the northern marsh orchid can be found on the reserve, as can evening primrose and pale toadflax.

Later in the walk you'll go through an impressive avenue of silver birch and past secluded pools frequented by various dragonflies, such as common darter, common hawker and broad-bodied chaser.

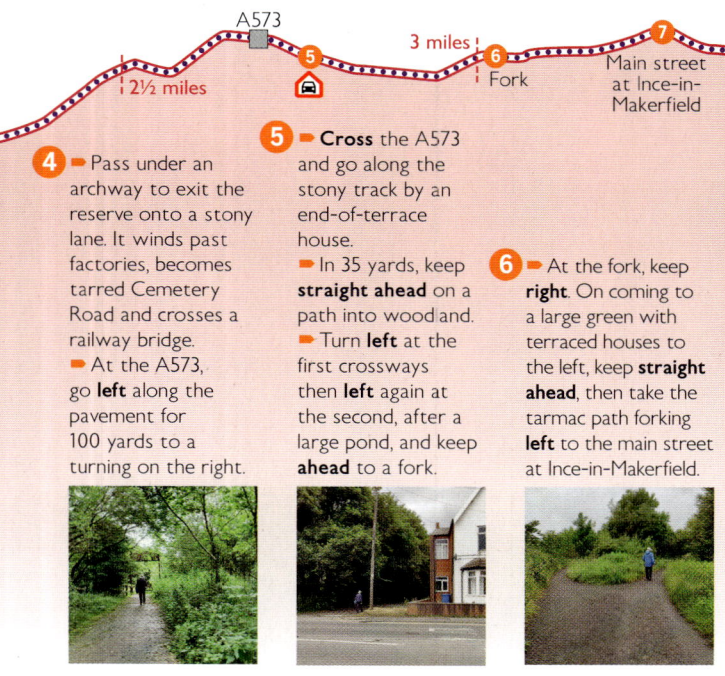

**4** ▬ Pass under an archway to exit the reserve onto a stony lane. It winds past factories, becomes tarred Cemetery Road and crosses a railway bridge.
▬ At the A573, go **left** along the pavement for 100 yards to a turning on the right.

**5** ▬ **Cross** the A573 and go along the stony track by an end-of-terrace house.
▬ In 35 yards, keep **straight ahead** on a path into woodland.
▬ Turn **left** at the first crossways then **left** again at the second, after a large pond, and keep **ahead** to a fork.

**6** ▬ At the fork, keep **right**. On coming to a large green with terraced houses to the left, keep **straight ahead**, then take the tarmac path forking **left** to the main street at Ince-in-Makerfield.

**Broad-bodied chaser**

**Top left**: pale toadflax
**Top right**: bittern
**Above**: northern marsh orchid

**7** ▶ Cross the road **diagonally left** to the signposted footpath opposite.
▶ After passing under a railway bridge, ignore paths to the left and right, and keep **forwards** to a footbridge over the Leeds & Liverpool Canal in 250 yards.

**8** ▶ **Cross** the bridge and turn **left** along the towpath. This brings the route to the canal junction at ❷.
▶ This time, go **straight ahead** for ⅓ mile to turn **right** by the Wigan Dry Dock, retracing steps to the car park.

**Walk 3** Wigan Pier and The Flashes

# WALK 4

## JUMBLES COUNTRY PARK AND TURTON TOWER

This is a fine walk in the once-industrial Bradshaw valley, set among the splendid rural Pennine scenery of Jumbles Country Park. Good paths lead round the reservoir, flanked by woodland, and there's a climb to see the 700-year-old Turton Tower, where you can view two mysterious skulls. The route passes through quiet, medieval Chapeltown before returning through Ousel Nest Meadows, a local nature reserve, to Jumbles and well-deserved tea and cake from the country park café.

### OS information
SD 736140
Explorer 287

| | |
|---|---|
| **Distance** | 3.75 miles/6km |
| **Time** | 2¼ hours |
| **Start/Finish** | Jumbles Country Park |
| **Parking** | BL2 4JS Waterfold car park (charge) |
| **Public toilets** | In the car park |
| **Cafés/pubs** | Visitor centre café near 🚶; Woodland Café, Turton Tower; Chetham Arms, Chapeltown |
| **Terrain** | Firm gravel reservoir path; cobbled streets; pavement; stony track; grassy path |

| | |
|---|---|
| **Hilliness** | One climb to, and descent from, Turton Tower |
| **Footwear** | Year round  |
| **Public transport** | Bee Network bus service 480, Bolton to Bury, stops on Bradshaw Road (A676), opposite the country park's access lane, 500 yards from ⓘ: tfgm.com; national rail services to Bromley Cross, just over ⅓ mile from ⑦: nationalrail.co.uk |
| **Accessibility** | Wheelchairs and pushchairs along the reservoir shore path ⓘ to ① |
| **Dogs** | Welcome dog friendly around the reservoir but keep on leads ① to ⑥. Two stiles |

**Did you know?** Turton Tower owner James Kay insisted that, if the railway were to pass through his estate, the necessary bridge would have to be designed to his specifications. The elegant castellated bridge passed after ④ is the result, designed in 1847 by Terence Flanagan.

**Local legend** Two skulls rest on a large family bible in a room often referred to as the chapel in Turton Tower. Previously, when the skulls have been separated, bad things happened. Long ago, or so the story goes, the landowner's daughter at Bradshaw Hall fell in love with a farmhand. Alas, the brother of the girl found out and murdered the farmhand. The girl died from a broken heart. Although separated in life, they must rest together in death.

Walk 4 Jumbles Country Park and Turton Tower 35

# STORIES BEHIND THE WALK

☆ **Chapeltown** A largely Georgian and Victorian hill village, Chapeltown is dominated by the spired church of St Anne's. The old stone-built Chetham's Arms pub is named after Hugh Chetham, the Manchester merchant who once lived in Turton Tower. A cobbled back road used in the walk passes beneath the church and an old bank, and crosses the railway near what was once a station.

☆ **Jumbles Reservoir** The name Jumbles derives from a term for a wooded ravine. Jumbles Reservoir was formed by damming the Bradshaw Brook. It was opened in 1971 by Queen Elizabeth II, and was intended to guarantee a water supply to the rivers Croal and Irwell, downstream. Today, the reservoir is part of the Jumbles Country Park, which includes a sailing club, recreational paths around the shoreline and the Ousel Nest Meadows local nature reserve.

☆ Jumbles Reservoir

Jumbles Country Park

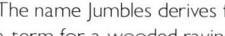

Bridge — ½ mile — Steps — Stile onto B6391

**Waterfold car park**

- Leave the car park by passing **left** of the toilet block then keep **ahead** on a wide track past the café. Walk with Jumbles Reservoir on your left for just over ½ mile to a bridge at its northern end.

**1** ▶ Turn **left** to cross the bridge and then leave the reservoir track by climbing the path (60 steps) up the hillside and through the woods ahead.

▶ Beyond the trees, a clear field path continues for 350 yards to a roadside stile.

**2** ▶ Climb over the stile, **cross** the road (B6391) and turn **right** along the pavement.

▶ In 275 yards, come to a road junction with three possible options ahead.

36 Short Walks Made Easy

## 🏠 Turton Tower

There has been a manor at Turton since the 1200s, part of the Barony of Manchester. The fortified pele tower you see today dates from 1420, built by the Orrell family, and has walls four feet thick. It was much extended as a manor house in the 16th and 17th centuries, and later became the residence of Humphrey Chetham (of the School of Music fame, see Walk 1). It's now owned by Blackburn with Darwen Council and is open to visitors to enjoy.

## ☆ Horrobin Bleach-works

The site of one of Bolton's oldest bleach-works, Horrobin Mill dates to around 1780. As the Victorian cotton industry flourished the bleach-works expanded. Entwistle Reservoir and then Wayoh Reservoir were constructed to supply water to the industry. The Horrobin Mill closed in 1941 and was demolished several years later. Submerged after Jumbles Reservoir was built, the mill foundations sometimes reappear in times of drought.

mile | ③ Station Road | ☆ Chapeltown | 1½ miles | ④ Gate | ☆ Castellated railway bridge

**③** ▪ Bear **left** along cobbled Station Road.
▪ Follow the road as it bends **left**, walk over a level-crossing and, immediately after, stay **left** to pass through a gate onto a rising field path, climbing to a gate and crossways at the top.

**④** ▪ Pass through the gate and turn **left** along a stony track.
▪ Go **left** at the junction in 400 yards, then over a castellated railway bridge to pass Turton Tower.
▪ At the track's end, turn **right** along the B6391 pavement for 300 yards to Horrobin Lane (left).

Walk 4 Jumbles Country Park and Turton Tower

# NATURE NOTES

Kestrels patrol the skies above Jumbles and you may spot a sparrowhawk in the woods, along with less predatory birds such as the great spotted woodpecker and nuthatch. There are wildfowl on the reservoir, including coot and mallard.

Cormorants are large, shiny black waterbirds, often seen with their wings held out to dry. They are proficient divers, with their webbed feet powering them beneath the surface.

The beautiful five-petalled, pink-flowered red campion is prolific in the country park. It can be found in lightly shaded woodland, in hedgerows and pastures like Ousel Nest Meadow. The male and female flowers of the red campion grow on separate plants and are important for pollinating insects like meadow brown butterflies. The plant is a strong indicator of ancient woodland.

The dog rose, which has pretty pink blooms that arrive in May and June, is a climber that uses hooked prickles to latch onto other plants in the hedgerow. In September, its bright red oval rose hips appear in small clusters.

**Top**: sparrowhawk
**Middle**: nuthatch
**Bottom**: coot

### 5
- Turn **left** along the cobbled Horrobin Lane.
- In 200 yards, fork **left**, signed Jumbles Sailing Club.
- Continue for another 125 yards to a bridge on the right, over an arm of the reservoir.

### 6
- Turn **right** and cross the bridge, passing to the **right** of the sailing club.
- In just under ½ mile, beyond a stable block and house, the path becomes a tarred road (Grange Road).
- Carry on for 500 yards to a gate and fingerpost (left).

**Mallards in flight**

Above: kestrel
Below: red campion

Jumbles Country Park
Grange Road

3 miles

Ousel Nest Meadows

Gate and fingerpost

3½ miles

Steps

Bridge

Waterfold car park

**7** ⇒ Go **left** through the gate onto a clear path that soon swings **left** through Ousel Nest Meadows Nature Reserve.

⇒ The path rakes down the hillside to cross a bridge below the reservoir dam before climbing 21 steps towards the top of the dam.

**8** ⇒ At a junction at the top of the steps, go **straight ahead** then take the wider of two paths bearing **right** and climbing back up to the car park.

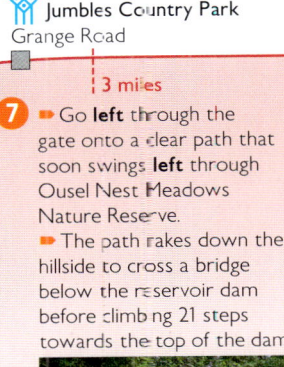

Walk 4  Jumbles Country Park and Turton Tower   39

Opposite (clockwise): long-tailed tit; whooper swan; Canada goose
This page (clockwise): bulrushes; common sandpiper; moorhen feeding chick; grey squirrel

# WALK 5

## IRWELL VALE TO RAMSBOTTOM

This linear walk starts from pretty Irwell Vale, its cottage gardens adorned with roses and colourful borders, and heads for Ramsbottom along the trackbed of the dismantled Accrington branch of the East Lancashire Railway, which passes through avenues of birch, sycamore and oak. In Ramsbottom, you can catch an East Lancashire Railway steam or vintage diesel train back through the valley to the start, where the Irwell Vale Chapel café serves lovely home-made cakes.

⚠ Check the railway timetable before setting off: eastlancsrailway.org.uk

### OS information
SD 792201
Explorer 287

**Distance**
2.7 miles/4.3km

**Time**
1½ hours

**Start** Irwell Vale
**Finish** Ramsbottom

**Parking** BL0 0QG
Irwell Vale Station car park

**Public toilets**
The Chapel café, Irwell Vale; Nuttall Park, Ramsbottom

**Cafés/pubs**
The Chapel café, Irwell Vale; village shop café, Stubbins; Ramsbottom

**Terrain**
Village streets and country lanes; former railway trackbed; grassy bridleway

**Did you know?** William and Daniel Grant, 19th-century industrialists who came to Ramsbottom, are reputed to be the inspiration for the Cheeryble brothers in Charles Dickens' book *Nicholas Nickleby*.

**Local legend** The East Lancashire Railway has its own ghost, 'Billy the Guard', who is said to stalk the waiting room between platforms three and four at Bury's Bolton Street Station; but the ghost is sometimes seen elsewhere on the line, as well as in the train carriages. Billy has also appeared in visitors' photos, usually asleep in his uniform.

**Hilliness**
Mostly flat, with one short ramp at ❶

**Footwear**
Winter 🥾
Spring/Summer/Autumn 👟

**Public transport**
East Lancashire Railway, for the return from Ramsbottom Station: eastlancsrailway.org.uk

**Accessibility**
Wheelchair and pushchair friendly 🚶 to ❸

**Dogs**
Welcome, but keep on leads after ❸ (livestock). One stile; three narrow kissing-gates

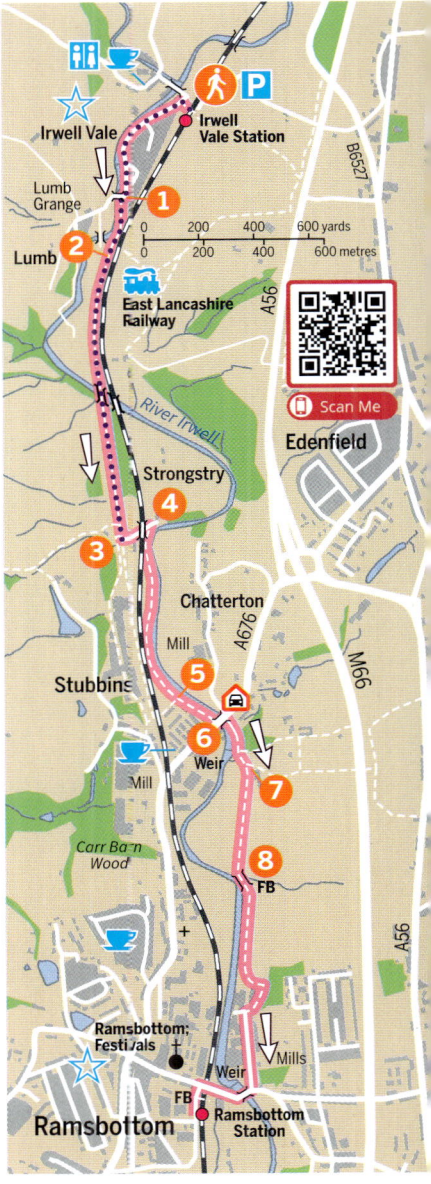

Walk 5 Irwell Vale to Ramsbottom

# STORIES BEHIND THE WALK

**East Lancashire Railway** Originally opened in 1848, after the Beeching report of the 1960s the last passenger train completed its journey in 1972. Coal trains ceased in 1980. However, in 1987, after much hard endeavour from the East Lancashire Railway Preservation Society, the line was reopened as a heritage railway on just four miles of track between Bury and Ramsbottom. Now the line operates between Heywood and Rawtenstall, and runs a fascinating transport museum near their Bury station (eastlancsrailway.org.uk).

**Irwell Vale** The village of Irwell Vale was founded when John Bowker, a wealthy Manchester merchant, built a woollen fulling mill by the banks of the Irwell in 1801. In the 1830s, he added a cotton mill on the other bank of the river. The first Methodist chapel was built in the 1850s, but was soon outgrown and a larger chapel was founded at the end of Bowker Street. The old chapel was converted into three houses: Chapel Row – cross the bridge near to see them.

Irwell Vale
East Lancashire Railway
Irwell Vale Station car park

Lumb Bridge ① ② ½ mile Ramp to former railway trackbed

River Irwell

➤ From the car park entrance, turn **left** along the road then **left** again along Meadow Park (also signed Chapel Row), which runs alongside the River Irwell.

➤ Continue by the river for ⅓ mile to the first bridge over it.

① ➤ As the road turns right over Lumb Bridge, leave it for a track on the **left** (the river still on your right).

➤ The path draws alongside the East Lancashire Railway line and a tarred track ramps up to join the trackbed of the old Accrington branch.

Short Walks Made Easy

## ⭐ Ramsbottom

Lying in the shadow of Holcombe Moor, Ramsbottom (the valley of the rams) is a thriving market town. The East Lancashire Railway is at its heart. Like many valleys in Pennine country, the Irwell was transformed during the Industrial Revolution when mills were built for spinning, weaving and printing. Sir Robert Peel, later British Prime Minister, was one of the famous entrepreneurs who drove the process forward and the Grant brothers continued this legacy.

## ⭐ Festivals

Ramsbottom is known for its events programmes and festivals, like East Lancashire Railway's 1940s Weekend. The town holds the Black Pudding World Championship annually at The Oaks pub. Participants have to hurl black puddings to dislodge a stack of Yorkshire puddings. The winner is the one who dislodges the most after three attempts. There's also a chocolate festival during the week before Easter.

**Irwell Viaduct**
**Old Accrington Branch Line**
1 mile
End of trackbed
Strongstry
Railway Bridge
River Irwell

**2** ▶ On joining the trackbed, follow a tarred path to the **left**. It leads through an avenue of broadleaved trees and across the River Irwell viaduct.
▶ 500 yards after the viaduct, meet the end of the trackbed where it is closed off.

**3** ▶ Turn **right** off the trackbed then **left** down a lane.
▶ At the bottom, go **left** under a bridge before passing through the houses of Strongstry and under another railway bridge.

# NATURE NOTES

Once one of the most polluted rivers in England, the Irwell is now a haven for wildlife. In this stretch you may see a kingfisher. These bright blue and orange birds are not much bigger than a robin and fly rapidly, close to the surface of the water, and hunt from low-hung branches. They eat small fish, such as minnows, and invertebrates, like dragonfly nymphs. Grey herons are ever-present along the River Irwell.

The shade-loving hart's tongue fern grows from the mossy stone walls lining the former railway trackbed. It has tongue-shaped glossy leaves with orange-brown spores on their undersides. This evergreen fern can often be found beneath trees and among rocks and streams.

In spring, you will smell the pungent aromas of ramsons (wild garlic). Large oval leaves grow from bulbs appearing in late winter. The plant has small, star-like white flowers with six petals. The blooms grow in large rounded clusters on a single, leafless stalk. Like bluebells, they usually grow in large carpets on the woodland floor.

Bluebells

**4** ▸ Just after the bridge, fork **right** along a narrow path; this soon follows the riverbank. In winter, and after heavy rainfall, this is likely to be muddy.

▸ After ⅓ mile the riverside path reaches housing.

**5** ▸ At the houses, the path turns **right**, then **left**, enclosed by back garden fences.

▸ After another **left-right** zigzag, it comes to the road at Stubbins (A676).

▸ Turn **left** to cross the footbridge parallel to the main road.

**6** ▸ At the far end of the bridge, cross the main road with care, and go **straight ahead** onto a signed, wide track.

▸ This soon narrows to a stony path, river to the right, and leads to a path junction.

Kingfisher

**Above**: ramsons
**Below**: oak leaf

River Irwell        First industrial estate unit    Industrial estate road    River Irwell   2½ miles   Ramsbottom Station   Level crossing   Festivals

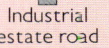

East Lancashire Railway

**7**
- At the junction, where the main path veers left, leave it for a path **ahead**.
- Go through a kissing-gate and follow the path towards a large barn.
- Passing through another kissing-gate, the path keeps to the **left** side of a large field and reaches a stiled bridge.

**8**
- **Cross** the bridge/stile. The path follows the Irwell again before veering **left**, rounding the first unit of an industrial estate.
- Emerging onto the estate road, turn **left** along it to a T-junction.
- Go **right** to a level crossing; Ramsbottom Station entrance is on the **left** for the train back to Irwell Vale.

Walk 5 Irwell Vale to Ramsbottom

WALK 6

# HOLLINGWORTH LAKE

Hollingworth Lake offers the perfect stroll. The paths, tracks and country lanes are flat and well surfaced. There are views of the lake and surrounding Pennine hills, and there's always wildlife to spot. Beginning on a narrow Victorian promenade, the walk continues with views to the rocky hill known as Blackstone Edge, which Daniel Defoe described as 'the Andes of the North'. The site of the once-famous Pavilion dance hall is passed before returning to the cafés and amusements of Smithy Bridge.

| OS information |
|---|
| SD 933150 Explorer OL21 |
| **Distance** 2.3 miles/3.7km |
| **Time** 1½ hours |
| **Start/Finish** Smithy Bridge |
| **Parking** OL15 0DQ Hollingworth Lake Bank car park, Smithy Bridge, Littleborough (charge) |
| **Public toilets** In the car park at 🚶; in the Pavilion at ⑤ |
| **Cafés/pubs** Lakeside Café; Pavilion Café; The Wine Press pub/restaurant; The Beach pub; Smithy Bridge |
| **Terrain** Gravelled lakeside tracks; quiet country lanes |
| **Hilliness** Level throughout |
| **Footwear** Year round  |

48  Short Walks Made Easy

### Public transport

Bus service 458, Rochdale to Stansfield, stops at 🚶: tfgm.com; national rail services to Smithy Bridge Station, about ½ mile from 🚶 nationalrail.co.uk

### Accessibility

Suitable for wheelchairs and pushchairs throughout

### Dogs

Welcome. No stiles

**Did you know?** Matthew Webb, the first man to swim the English Channel from Dover to Calais, regularly came to the cold waters of Hollingworth Lake to practice.

**Local legend** Some historians believe that Oliver Cromwell stayed in a small house known as Oliver's Cottage, near the Rake Inn on the Blackstone Edge Road. He was being pursued by an enemy in the Civil War, known as the Rake Cavalier, who was probably killed by Cromwell's Roundheads. The Cavalier is said to haunt the lanes around Hollingworth Lake. Apparently, he may be seen in full uniform, smiling and sometimes drunk.

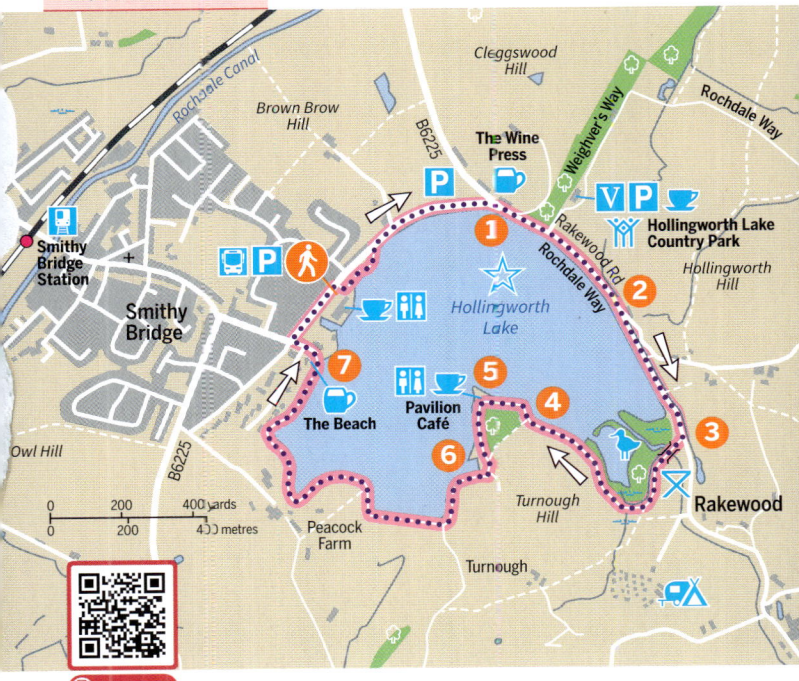

Walk 6 Hollingworth Lake 49

# STORIES BEHIND THE WALK

☆ **Hollingworth Lake**  Hollingworth Lake, built to supply water to the Rochdale Canal, was constructed in 1798, unusually, not in a valley but in a basin. It had dams on three sides. Being lower than the canal summit, a steam-powered water pump was installed to raise the water to a channel that fed the canal. The much higher Blackstone Edge and Chelburn reservoirs were built to supplement supply to the higher locks.

☆ **Building the Rochdale Canal**  Plans for the Rochdale Canal between Manchester and Sowerby Bridge in Yorkshire were first mooted in 1776 when James Brindley was asked to survey a route. The idea lay dormant until 1791 when John Rennie made a new survey. Local mill owners, worried about losing water supply for their factories, delayed its construction. However, solutions were found and the scheme was authorised in 1794.

The Wine Press

 Hollingworth Lake Country Park (left)

 Hollingworth Lake Bank car park

☆ **Hollingworth Lake**

½ mile

 Country Park Café

- With your back to the road, leave the leftmost car park for the shoreline path beyond the fish and chip shop by the slipway. The path with iron railings avoids the parallel road.
- Follow the path for ⅓ mile to The Wine Press pub.

**1** ➤ At the pub, the shoreline path rounds the top of the lake and joins a roadside pavement (Rakewood Road).
- In 150 yards, pass the entrance to Hollingworth Lake Country Park (café).
- In another 350 yards, reach a road fork.

50  Short Walks Made Easy

## ☆ The rise of tourism

The opening of the Manchester and Leeds Railway in 1839 brought tourism opportunities to the area. In the 1850s, mill owner Henry Newall and his engineer James Sladen leased the lake from the canal company. Hotels were built and two paddle steamers were operated. Rowing boats became a popular attraction. Hollingworth became known as the 'Weighvers Seaport'. In its heyday, crowds of up to 25,000 visited. The Pavilion on the south side of the lake would hold dances deep into the night, revellers often causing trouble for the locals.

## ☆ Military history

An army training camp for the Manchester Regiment was established in the nearby Ealees valley during World War I. Hotels at the lake were used for billeting wives and families of the soldiers. Many of the soldiers were sent to Gallipoli and died on the beaches there. In World War II, barges were placed in Blackstone Edge Reservoir (east of Littleborough) to prevent German sea planes from landing.

## ☆ Hollingworth Lake

**2** ............... **3** ............... | 1 mile
Road fork          Country park entrance

R a k e w o o d    R o a d

**2** ■ Remain next to the shoreline and continue along Rakewood Road for ¼ mile to the next turning on the right.

**3** ■ Leave Rakewood Road by branching **right** onto a country park lane, crossing a bridge, and following it past a children's play area.
■ After a sweeping right-hand bend, the lane meets the lakeside and runs on to a junction.

Walk 6 Hollingworth Lake  51

# NATURE NOTES

Mute swans are resident all year round while, in winter, they may be joined by whooper swans that have travelled across the North Atlantic from Iceland. The orange and black beak of the mute swan distinguishes it from the yellow and black bill of the whooper.

The grey heron, a tall wading bird with long legs, a long beak and with grey, black and white feathering, is a common sight. Its diet includes fish, but also small birds, voles, frogs and newts.

Often heard in the trees, chiffchaffs are small birds that are hard to spot. They are a common summer visitor from Africa, their distinctive and ceaseless 'chiff-chaff chiff-chaff chiff-chaff' call is a harbinger of spring.

If you're quiet, you may glimpse a roe deer in the woodland around the lake.

In summer, the lakesides are decorated with stands of foxglove, ragwort and ox-eye daisy. In Greek mythology, the ox-eye daisy was dedicated to Artemis, goddess of the moon.

Ox-eye daisy

☆ **Hollingworth Lake**

**4** Path junction

**5**  Pavilion Café

**6** Path junction beyond an old boating centre

1½ miles

**4** ▶ At the junction, keep **right** to stay with the shoreline. The winding lane passes a short path to a bird hide before coming to the site of the old Pavilion and its café.

**5** ▶ Go **left** round the café and, in 200 yards, pass to the **left** of an old boating centre to reach a path junction.

52  Short Walks Made Easy

Foxglove and ragwort

**Above**: chiffchaff
**Below**: grey heron

Top: roe deer Above: mute swan

The Beach

2 miles

Hollingworth Lake Bank car park

☆ H o l l i n g w o r t h   L a k e

**6** ▶ Turn **right** on a path that winds round the lake shoreline for ⅔ mile and comes to The Beach (pub), near 🚶.

**7** ▶ Angle **right** in front of the pub, walk through its car park and turn **right** along the road back to the starting point.

Walk 5  Hollingworth Lake

WALK 7

# DOVE STONE RESERVOIR

This walk is set in Greater Manchester's piece of the Peak District, where Saddleworth Moor towers above the Tame valley. It's a spectacular scene, lending itself to an easy walk around the lowest of four reservoirs – Dove Stone – filling two side valleys of the Tame. Shapely summits and crags surround the reservoir's shore path, while a delightful picnic spot awaits at the halfway point – eat a packed lunch while watching sailing dinghies racing across the water.

### OS information

🚶 SE 013033
Explorer OL1

**Distance**
2.8 miles/4.5km

**Time**
1¾ hours

**Start/Finish**
Dove Stone Reservoir

**Parking** OL3 7NE
Dove Stone Reservoir car park (charge)

**Public toilets**
In the car park

**Cafés/pubs**
Picnic benches; seasonal ice-cream van; The Clarence, Greenfield, 1 mile from 🚶

**Terrain**
Tarred or gravelled paths

54  Short Walks Made Easy

**Hilliness**
Fairly flat, with two short moderate climbs and one moderate descent

**Footwear**
Year round

**Public transport**
None; nearest bus stop at The Clarence, Greenfield, for services 180, Oldham; 350/357, Ashton-under-Lyne; and 352/357 Holmfirth: tgfm.com

**Accessibility**
Wheelchairs and pushchairs throughout; there are five gates operated by radar keys for larger, motorised mobility chairs

**Dogs**
Welcome but on leads (livestock). No stiles

**Did you know?** In 1981 King Taufa'ahau Tupou IV of Tonga visited Dove Stone Reservoir after attending the wedding of Prince Charles and Princess Diana. There's a commemoration stone built into the Yeoman Hey Dam wall.

**Local legend** In 2010, there were sightings of a large black beast around Greenfield and cases of lambs found mutilated. Farmer, Chris Crowther, discovered the first carcass near Dove Stone Reservoir but there were further sightings of the beast at Wessenden and other Saddleworth villages. There were reports in the news that this may have been a puma, although the Black Beast of Greenfield was never caught.

Scan Me

Walk 7  Dove Stone Reservoir  55

# STORIES BEHIND THE WALK

☆ **The Greenfield and Chew Valley Reservoirs** Yeoman Hey Reservoir was completed in 1880, Greenfield in 1902 and Chew, which at 1,600 feet above sea level was the highest in England at the time, in 1912. Dove Stone Reservoir came much later, in 1966. It had the last large dam built in Britain with a puddle-clay core and, unusually, there was no spillway to release excess water – instead a large bell-mouth shaft overflow is used to discharge water into a side tunnel.

☆ **The Moors Murderers** Saddleworth Moor made the news headlines in the 1960s with the infamous 'moors murders'. A young Mira Hindley had become besotted with Ian Brady and he encouraged her to collaborate with him in the 'perfect murders'. The child victims were all buried on the lonely moors above Dove Stone Reservoir. Hindley and Brady died in 2002 and 2017 respectively, and the burial site of one of their victims remains unknown.

① Path junction, just beyond a bridge — ½ mile

Sailing Club

☆ Dove Stone Reservoir

Dove Stone Reservoir car park

- From the car park, with your back to the reservoir, go **left** along the lane to the top of the dam, passing the toilets (right).
- Carry on for almost ½ mile, passing the sailing club (left), to a junction just beyond a bridge.

① ▪ Turn **left** off the lane to follow a stony track above the east side of the reservoir (water on the left), and beneath Dove Stone Rocks, for just over ½ mile to a fingerpost and fork.

Short Walks Made Easy

## ☆ Bill o' Jacks

Looking at the Ordnance Survey map you'll see the name Bill o' Jacks Plantation to the north of Yeoman Hey Reservoir. Bill o' Jacks was the nickname of the Moorcock Inn, which stood in a remote spot on Saddleworth Moor, not far from the plantation. The pub was owned by Bill Bradbury who lived there with his son Tom. On 2 April 1832 it was the scene of their brutal murders. Nobody was ever convicted of the crime and the pub was eventually demolished.

## ☆ Greenfield

The Romans built a road through Greenfield – one of several villages in the parish of Saddleworth – to link forts at Chester, Manchester and York. In the 17th century, the villages were home to hand-loom weavers and farmers. Industry boomed with the opening of the Huddersfield Narrow Canal, Thomas Telford's epic 3-mile-long Standedge Tunnel beneath the Pennines facilitating larger cotton and woollen spinning mills.

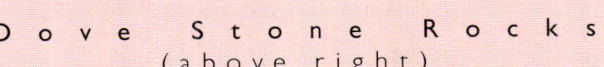

Fingerpost and fork
❷
1 mile

✗ (left)

# Dove Stone Rocks
## (above right)

**❷** ▪ At the fork, stay with the main track rather than descending left through woodland.
▪ Continue to a bridge at Ashway Gap in ⅓ mile.

**❸** ▪ Remain on the track over the bridge at Ashway Gap, an idyllic picnic site on the left.
▪ Follow the track to the next bridge in 275 yards.

Walk 7 Dove Stone Reservoir 57

# NATURE NOTES

The reservoirs were once surrounded by plantations of larch, spruce and pine, but these were in a poor state and are being replaced in a sensitive fashion by deciduous, broadleaved trees like rowan, silver birch and oak.

Among the new planting, ponds have been excavated to conserve palmate newts and many species of dragonfly.

The improved moorland edge habitat has benefited the ring ouzel, a member of the thrush family and similar in size to a blackbird. It's a summer visitor, with black plumage, a white collar and pale silvery wing panel.

Looking up to the skyline crags you may well see buzzards and ravens soaring on the thermals, as well as Britain's fastest bird, the peregrine falcon.

Meadow cranesbill can be found in the grassland around the lake; it grows in profusion at the picnic area near ❸, where its lovely blue flowers harmonise with the mauve flowers of field scabious.

Palmate newt

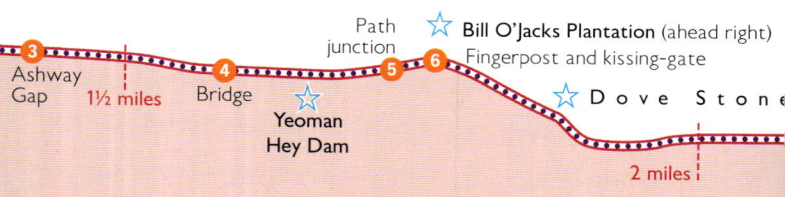

**4** ▸ **Cross** the bridge and turn **left** over the Yeoman Hey Dam to a path junction on the far side.

**5** ▸ Go **left** at the junction, following a tarred lane for 70 yards to a fork, fingerpost and kissing-gate on the left, overlooking the reservoir spillway.

**Top**: buzzard
**Bottom**: raven

**Top**: rowan berries
**Middle**: field scabious
**Bottom**: ring ouzel

Reservoir — Bell-mouth shaft overflow — Dove Stone Dam

2½ miles

**6** ► Fork **left** through the kissing-gate onto a descending stony track, which hugs the western shoreline of the reservoir for ½ mile before doubling back **left** to descend to a kissing-gate at the top of Dove Stone Dam.

**7** ► Go through the kissing-gate and follow the path across the dam for ⅓ mile before turning **right** at the end onto the lane back to the car park.

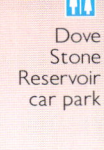

Dove Stone Reservoir car park

Walk 7  Dove Stone Reservoir    59

Opposite (clockwise): Entwistle's Deli, Ramsbottom; Tree Tops Café, Sale Water Park
This page (clockwise): Visitor centre café, Etherow Country Park; Jackson's Boat, Sale Water Park; Pavilion Café, Hollingworth Lake; Dunham Massey Farm ice-cream shop; Turton Tower Woodland Café

# WALK 8

# ETHEROW
# COUNTRY PARK

CATCH A BUS

| OS information |
|---|
| ⚲ SJ 965908<br>Explorers 277, OL1 |
| **Distance**<br>2.6 miles/4.2km |
| **Time**<br>1½ hours |
| **Start/Finish**<br>Compstall |
| **Parking** SK6 5JD<br>Etherow Country<br>Park car park,<br>George Street,<br>Compstall (charge) |
| **Public toilets**<br>In the car park;<br>Etherow Park Weir,<br>near ❷ |
| **Cafés/pubs**<br>Etherow County<br>Park café; Potting<br>Shed Café/garden<br>centre; Andrew<br>Arms, Compstall |

Lying between the moorland of the Dark Peak and the conurbation of Manchester, Etherow Country Park couldn't be more different to either. Here, the River Etherow flows in a steep-sided, verdant valley cloaked with lovely woodland. The man-made lakes have blended splendidly with their surroundings. This route can be divided into two: a circuit of the main mill pond provides a flat, easy-paced walk suitable for all users; the extension (for walkers without wheels) takes you deeper into the forest.

62   Short Walks Made Easy

### Terrain
Surfaced paths, lanes; field and woodland paths

### Hilliness
♿ The lake circuit is flat. The woodland route is undulating, with moderate climbs

### Footwear
Year round 👟

### 🚌 Public transport
Bus service 38, Stockport to Marple, with stop near 🚶: tgfm.com

### ♿ Accessibility
Wheelchair and pushchair friendly 🚶 to ❷, returning via a shortcut to ❻

### 🐕 Dogs
Welcome but keep on leads. No stiles

**Did you know?** Many of the streets in Compstall village are named after the local early 19th-century entrepreneur and industrialist George Andrew and members of his family. Examples near the start of the walk include George and Montagu streets, and Edith Terrace.

**Local legend** The area around the banks of the River Goyt, just to the south of Compstall, is believed to be haunted by King Charles I and by the daughter of Roundhead Henry Bracshaw. The daughter fell in love with a Royalist officer who would visit Marple Hall during the Civil War. The officer was murdered by drowning in the Goyt after being discovered at the hall. The daughter died of a broken heart. And King Charles I? Well, a certain relative, John Bradshaw, signed the king's death warrant. The hall? Well, that is long demolished.

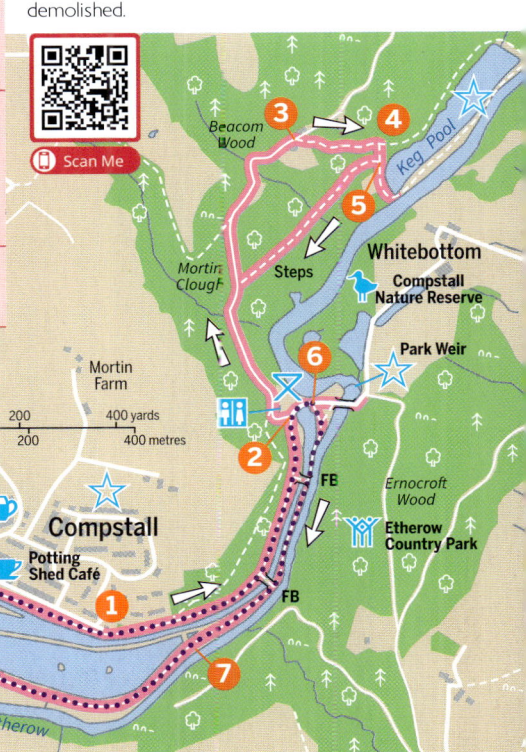

Walk 8 Etherow Country Park  63

# STORIES BEHIND THE WALK

### ☆ Compstall, the beginnings
Before the Industrial Revolution, Compstall was a market place for farmers to trade their sheep. To seal their deals they would spit on their palms and hit the Touch Stone – a rock deposited by a retreating ice sheet at the end of the last ice age, known as a glacial erratic. You can see it next to a wooden marker post on a small green on the corner of Compstall Road and George Street.

### ☆ Compstall, the mill town
George Andrew brought industry to Compstall in the 1820s when he built a water-powered cotton mill, and the associated reservoirs and infrastructure to power great water wheels. Andrew also built a printworks and houses for his 800 workers, along with a church, school and reading rooms. It was one of the first villages in the country to have gas lighting and the first in the region to have a Co-op store. The mills declined in the 20th century, and the last one closed in 1966.

 Lake shore path | Lane | ½ mile | Lane beside narrowing lake |  Turn right

 **Etherow Country Park**

 Etherow Country Park car park

▬ From the car park, pass in front of the visitor centre and follow the wide path by the lake shore for ¼ mile to reach a lane.

❶ ▬ Go **right** along the lane for almost ½ mile, with the narrowing lake on your right, until the lane forks (fingerpost) at Weir House.

### 🐦 Compstall Nature Reserve

Set within the country park, Compstall Nature Reserve was designated as a Site of Special Scientific Interest (SSSI) in 1977, mainly for its diverse habitats, which include open water, tall fen, reed swamp and mixed deciduous ancient woodland. This wildlife refuge has a bird hide overlooking the River Etherow.

### 🙌 Etherow Country Park

Founded in 1968, Etherow Country Park was one of the first of its kind in England. The River Etherow, which has tumbled down from the peatland slopes of Bleaklow, flows through the park. Here George Andrew's mill ponds feature in a lovely wooded setting. The pretty Keg Pool, at the far end of the park, was excavated as a fishing lake by George Andrew. Perhaps the centrepiece is the huge Etherow Park Weir, near ⑥.

Beacom Wood — 1 mile | ③ House in Beacom Wood — Path junction before Keg Pool — ④ Keg Pool — 🐦 Compstall Nature Reserve — ⑤ Woodland Path

**②** ➤ 🔄 Turn **right** to view the weir (125 yards). On the way, note that the first path right, at ⑥ (picnic site), is your return route.
➤ Otherwise, turn **left** (lane signed Keg Wood and Sunny Corner).
➤ Keep **left** at a path turning in 350 yards continuing to a house in Beacom Wood.

**③** ➤ At the far side of the house, turn **right** then, after a few paces, take the **left** fork. Continue for 175 yards on a grassy way descending and narrowing to a path junction just before Keg Pool.

# NATURE NOTES

The mixed woodland of Etherow Country Park dates back to 1600 and includes oak, silver birch, sycamore, hawthorn and hazel on valley slopes, and willow and alder in the wetlands around Keg Pool.

Goldcrest, long-tailed tit, great spotted woodpecker and nuthatch can regularly be seen in the woodland, while moorhens, grey herons, little grebes, coots, kingfishers and Canada geese may well be spotted around the lakes.

Speckled wood, comma, peacock and orange-tip butterflies are seen along the pathways.

In summer, you'll notice that the park is cloaked with Himalayan balsam, a plant originally introduced to Britain from the Himalayas in 1839. It's a huge plant (up to 8 feet in height) with beautiful pink blooms, much liked by bees. Unfortunately, it spreads very quickly and tends to out-compete other wildflowers. Each spring volunteers come to the park to control but not eradicate the most intrusive patches.

Himalayan balsam

Flight of steps
1½ miles

Park Weir
Footpath

## Etherow Country Park

**4** ▶ Take the **right** fork at the junction, very soon passing the return path (right); but first, keep **forward** to a seating area next to the lake.
▶ After enjoying the scene, head back to the path turning for the return.

**5** ▶ Go **left** along a woodland path (narrow in places).
▶ It crosses a wooden bridge before climbing a flight of steps to rejoin the lane used earlier.
▶ Turn **left**, back along the lane to the junction **2**, there going **left** for 125 yards to the weir.

**Left**: orange-tip
**Above**: goat willow
**Bottom left**: goldcrest
**Below**: peacock

## Etherow Country Park

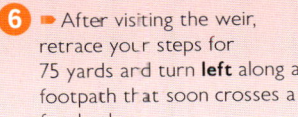

River Etherow — 2 miles
Lake shore path
Three-way fork
Etherow Country Park car park — 2½ miles

**6** ▶ After visiting the weir, retrace your steps for 75 yards and turn **left** along a footpath that soon crosses a footbridge.
▶ The path continues along a slender isthmus between the River Etherow and a narrow lake for ⅓ mile to a three-way fork.

**7** ▶ At the junction, take the **leftmost** of three paths to join a wide stony track alongside the country park's main lake. This leads back to the start.

**Walk 8** Etherow Country Park

# WALK 9

TAKE A TRAM

# SALE WATER PARK

The valley of the River Mersey meanders lazily through a pleasant green corridor between the suburbs of Greater Manchester. The river is particularly pleasant around the Sale and Chorlton water parks, where a significant effort has been made to create diverse wildlife havens. The walk begins at the historic Jackson's Boat (pub) and follows the banks of the Mersey before delving between Sale Water Park's lake and the pools and wetlands of the Broad Ees Dole Nature Reserve.

## OS information

SJ 810926
Explorer 277

**Distance**
2.6 miles/4.2km

**Time**
1½ hours

**Start/Finish**
Sale Water Park

**Parking** M33 2LX
Jackson's Boat (Sale Water Park) car park, Rifle Road (charge)

**Public toilets**
Visitor centre, at Tree Tops Café

**Cafés/pubs**
Tree Tops Café; Jackson's Boat (pub)

**Terrain**
Well-surfaced paths

**Hilliness**
Mostly flat; one ramp at 🚶

**Footwear**
Year round

**Public transport**
Tram service to Sale Water Park Station (Navy Line), 350 yards from 🚶 and 200 yards from 6. tfgm.com

**Accessibility**
Stony ramp at 🚶 too steep for manual wheelchairs, but access throughout should be possible for powered wheelchairs; suitable for all-terrain pushchairs.

**Dogs**
Welcome. No stiles

**Did you know?** Before the creation of Greater Manchester, the River Mersey was the long-adopted boundary between Lancashire and Cheshire. The Jackson's Boat pub, being on the south bank of the river, ought logically to have been on the Cheshire side. However, due to an anomaly caused by changes in the river's course over the centuries, it remained in Lancashire.

**Local legend** Barlow Hall, near neighbouring Chorlton Water Park, has a reputation for being haunted. Sir Edward Barlow, known as Ambrose, was born at Barlow Hall in 1585, and was ordained as a Benedictine priest. He was hanged for his Catholic faith at Lancaster Gaol and was later canonised by Pope Paul VI. His ghost is said to haunt the upper floors of the hall.

⚠ Some of the paths are impassable if the Sale Ees Sluice Gate is open. Flood warning notices will be displayed, but check before setting out: riverlevels.uk/greater-manchester-sale-waterpark

To avoid closed paths, take the upper flood bank path 🚶 to ① and follow the alternative route shown on this map to ⑤ and rejoin the described walk at Tree Tops Café.

Walk 9 Sale Water Park

# STORIES BEHIND THE WALK

☆ **Before the Lake** In the Middle Ages, the lands around the Mersey were lush meadows known as ees (lands liable to flooding). This was mixed farming countryside.

Sale Old Hall once stood at the south side of Rifle Road. Built in the early 1600s for the Massey family, it was rebuilt in the 1840s and demolished in the 1920s. All that remained was the lodge – now the Sale Golf Club's clubhouse – and a dovecote – relocated to Walkden Gardens, Sale, when the M60 was built.

☆ **Sale Water Park**
For its construction in the 1970s, an embankment was needed to raise the M60 above the Mersey's flood plain. A gravel pit was excavated to provide the material for the embankment and then flooded to form the lake. Sale Water Park was opened in 1979 and includes leisure facilities such as yachting, and swimming, with areas set aside for nature. Since then, Broad Ees Dole Nature Reserve has been developed into a wetland for wildlife.

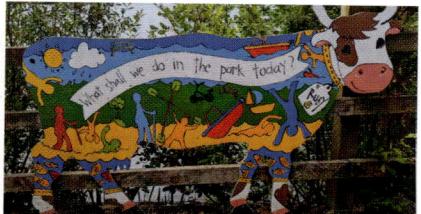

Jackson's Boat

☆ Sale Ees Sluice Gate          ½ mile

☆ River Mersey

- Facing Jackson's Boat pub, turn **left** and go up the ramp to the track running alongside the River Mersey ⚠ see note on page 69.
- Turn **left** along the riverside for almost 1½ miles to a path junction in front of a tram line bridge.

**1** - Approaching the bridge (Barfoot Bridge), fork **left** at the path junction and then turn **left**, away from the river, to continue 70 yards to the next path junction (Sale Water Park sign).

70  Short Walks Made Easy

## ☆ Sale Ees Sluice Gate

One of the first structures encountered on the walk is the Sale Ees Sluice Gate, near Jackson's Bridge. The colourful mural decorating it was designed and painted by artists Russell Meehan and Dan Birbeck, along with students from Stretford Grammar School. When the River Mersey reaches a level that makes it likely to flood, the sluice is opened to let the excess water flow along a channel behind into Sale Water Park.

## ☕ Jackson's Boat

Originally the Old Greyhound, the inn was built in 1663. It was used as a meeting place for Jacobites during the rebellion of the 18th century. A local farmer, known as Jackson, began operating a ferry across the river to the inn, which is how it got its name. The ferry ceased in 1816 when a wooden bridge was constructed on the site of the current crossing. The inn became the Bridge Inn although locals called it Jackson's Boat.

## ☆ River Mersey

⋮ 1 mile

**②** ▪ Go **left** again. Follow the path round Sale Water Park lake (right), passing a brick-built bird hide and the smaller Broad Ees Dole lakes (left).
▪ Continue beneath the Mersey's flood embankment as the path becomes Cow Lane; carry on to a lane fork.

## 🐦 Broad Ees Dole Nature Reserve

**③** ▪ Fork **right**, away from the embankment. Continue on Cow Lane, ignoring all side paths, to a bridge (stone parapets) and brightly painted, cow-shaped murals.

Walk 9 Sale Water Park

# NATURE NOTES

The mudflats of Broad Ees Dole are ideal for birds like snipe and ringed plovers. Migratory birds, such as common sandpiper and redshank, feed alongside cormorant, grey heron, coot, moorhen and teal. Canada geese are prolific on the big lake and there is a breeding pair of mute swans. Jays, Britain's most colourful crow, inhabit the woodland.

The emperor is Britain's biggest dragonfly. Males have a blue body; females are green. The emperor dragonfly is always on the move, catching and often eating its prey on the wing. It likes well-vegetated ponds and lakes, canals and slow-flowing rivers.

Hibernating in winter as an adult insect, brimstones are often the first butterflies to be seen in spring. The male is the colour of butter, while the female is a pale green. Buckthorn, which is abundant in the wetland, is the butterfly's larval food plant.

Banks of colourful rosebay willowherb line the watercourses in summer.

Redshank

Path junction; Sale Water Park sign

Broad Ees Dole Nature Reserve

Barfoot Bridge ahead

1½ miles

Path below the flood embankment

**4** ▪ Stay on the tarred Cow Lane (unless the flood warning gates are closed).
▪ Continue for 300 yards to a turning on the left, the red roof of Tree Tops Café visible.

**5** ▪ Turn **left** on a path that passes behind the café.
▪ The path carries on, drawing alongside Rifle Road, keeping parallel with it to the far end of a large car park, by a fingerpost and path junction.

**Top:** emperor dragonfly
**Middle:** brimstone
**Bottom:** rosebay willowherb

**Top: common snipe**
**Bottom: ringed plover**

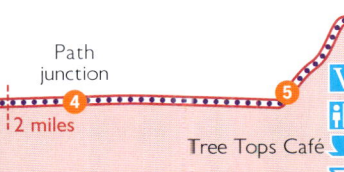

**6** ▶ Just beyond the car park, where the road turns right, keep **forward** along the footpath, signed to the River Mersey, to a wooden gateway in 250 yards.

**7** ▶ Just beyond the wooden gateway, fork **right** and follow the path back to the Jackson's Boat car park.

# WALK 10

## DUNHAM MASSEY

This easy-paced walk takes in beautiful countryside between Cheshire and Greater Manchester. Setting out along a lovely disused railway path, the walk crosses the Dunham Massey Estate. After a while, you'll recognise the estate's regal maroon colour on the windows, doors and signs. Fine village pubs line the route to the impressive mansion, which dates back to medieval times. In the estate parkland you may well be able to see fallow deer. The walk finishes on the Bridgewater Canal (nationaltrust.org.uk/visit/cheshire-greater-manchester/dunham-massey).

### OS information

🚶 SJ 750888
Explorers 268, 276

**Distance**
5.2 miles/8.3 km

**Time**
3 hours

**Start/Finish**
Oldfield Brow, Altrincham

**Parking** WA14 5RF
Trans Pennine Trail car park, Seamons Road

**Public toilets**
None; toilets at Dunham Massey Hall (NT) and, for customers, at each of the pubs en route

**Cafés/pubs**
National Trust café; Rope & Anchor, and Vine Inn, Dunham Woodhouses; Swan with Two Nicks, Little Bollington; Axe & Cleaver, Dunham Town

**Terrain**
Former railway trackbed; country lane; canal towpath; public footpath across the Dunham Massey Estate

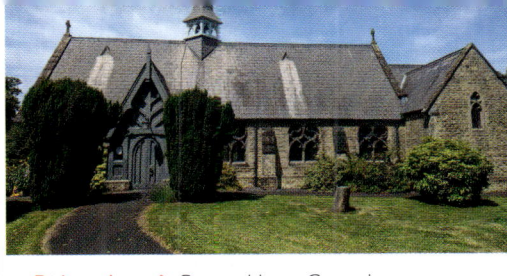

**Hilliness**
Mostly flat or gently undulating

**Footwear**
Year round

 **Public transport**
Bus service 280, Altrincham Interchange to Dunham Town, with stops near ① and Vine Inn: arrivabus.co.uk/north-west

 **Accessibility**
Powered wheelchair and all-terrain pushchair friendly from ① to ③ and from ④ to end; if visiting Dunham Massey Hall, follow alternative route from ②

 **Dogs**
Welcome but keep on leads across Dunham Massey parkland (deer). Two stiles

**Did you know?** George Harry Grey, the seventh Earl of Stamford, married twice: firstly to a shoemaker's daughter then to a circus performer. His peers around Dunham Massey didn't approve and this led to him leaving the family seat to live at Enville Hall in Staffordshire.

**Local legend** In the late 18th century, an architect involved in the refurbishing of Dunham Massey Hall is said to have been pushed to his death. Apparently, his unhappy spirit roams the corridors of the hall. The Oak Bedroom and Stamford Bathroom are also locations for paranormal activity. Visitors have noted sudden temperature drops, and have felt invisible hands around their necks.

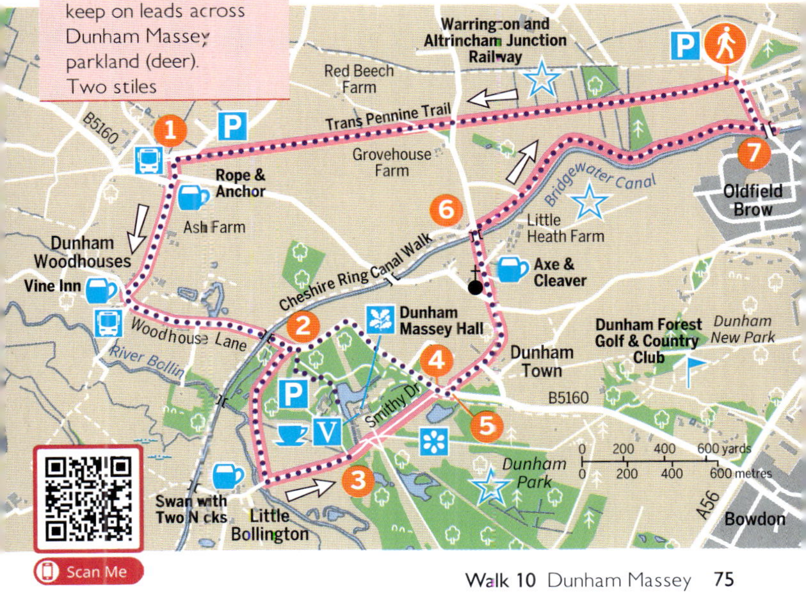

# STORIES BEHIND THE WALK

**Dunham Massey Hall** Construction of the original house was started by Sir George Booth, first Baronet and High Sheriff of both Lancashire and Cheshire, in the early 17th century, but it was completed after his death by his grandson George. In the 1730s, the hall was completely redesigned by architect John Norris and, later that century, Capability Brown landscaped the park. In 1976 Roger Grey, the tenth Earl of Stamford, left the estate to the National Trust, who manage it today.

**Military duties**
In 1917, Penelope Grey, Countess of Stamford, sanctioned the Red Cross to use the hall as the Stamford Military Hospital. It was run by Sister Catherine Bennett. Lady Stamford's daughter, Lady Jane Grey, later trained in the hospital to be a nurse. In World War II, the eastern part of the hall was requisitioned by the United States Army as a base, but was later used as a prisoner of war camp, with 6,000 Germans held in over 200 buildings.

**Warrington and Altrincham Junction Railway**

Trans Pennine Trail car park | ½ mile | 1 mile

## Trans Pennine Trail

- With your back to the car park entrance, go **forward** through the gap by the cycle restrictor and turn **left** along the wide, former railway trackbed – the Trans Pennine Trail.
- Walk for 1½ miles to a gateway, just past a car park.

**1** - Pass through the gateway and turn **left** along Station Road. Go **straight on** at the next two junctions, passing the Rope & Anchor.
- Bend **left** beyond the Vine Inn along Woodhouse Lane. After passing under a canal bridge, look for a turning in 100 yards (right).

Short Walks Made Easy

## ☆ Warrington and Altrincham Junction Railway

The opening 1½ miles of this walk is along the trackbed of the former Warrington and Altrincham Junction Railway, built in 1853. It linked with other railway lines to ensure that there was a through route from Manchester, and had various owners through the years, culminating with London Midland Scottish before the nationalised British Railways. The line was closed to passengers in 1962 but continued as a freight line until 1985.

## ☆ Bridgewater Canal

Considered to be the first true canal constructed in England, the Bridgewater Canal was built for Francis Egerton, the third Duke of Bridgewater, to transport coal from his mine in Worsley to the ever expanding towns of the north. It is 39 miles long, running from Manchester to Leigh. James Brindley's design was originally to have no locks, which wasted water, although in the end there was a double lock at Pomona Docks in Salford.

Gateway/Station Road — Rope & Anchor — 1½ miles — Station Road — Dunham Woodhouses — Vine Inn — 2 miles — Woodhouses Lane — Road passes under Bridgewater Canal — Restricted byway — Keep forward 50 yards to NT hall entrance — 2½ miles

**2** ▶ At a restricted byway sign, keep **forward** 50 yards to Dunham Massey (NT) entrance.
▶ Otherwise, turn **right** to follow the lane for almost ½ mile to a T-junction (Bollington Mill).
▶ Turn **left** along a wide track for just over 400 yards to a gate/stile.

**3** ▶ **Cross** the stile and enter the parkland at Dunham Massey.
▶ Maintain your direction along the track (Smithy Drive) across the park, passing in front of the hall and ignoring all turnings to reach another gate/stile, with a road beyond.

Walk 10 Dunham Massey

# NATURE NOTES

You may well see fallow deer in Dunham Park. This medium-sized deer has a gingery-brown coat with white spots and a white rump. The species was originally from Asia but was introduced to England in the 11th century by Norman barons for the purpose of hunting.

There's a seasonal hedgehog trail through Dunham Massey. Seven rare species of beetle have been found, so do look around the log piles left in the park to see what bugs you can find. The garden flowers attract butterflies such as red admiral and painted lady.

The most common waterfowl on the canal are moorhen, coot and mallard. Most mallard are resident birds, but in winter migrants also arrive from Iceland and Northern Europe.

Hedge bindweed has large heart-shaped leaves and velvety, white trumpet-like flowers which appear between June and September. It is a perennial plant with stems that die back in the winter to rhizomes, which lie just below the surface. It is extremely deep-rooted.

Young hedgehog

**4** ▪ **Cross** the stile to leave the Dunham Massey grounds and turn **right** along the road for just less than 100 yards to the first turning on the left.

**5** ▪ Turn **left** at the junction, signed to Dunham Town Crematorium.
▪ Keep **straight on** at the first junction and **ahead** again by a small church, and continue for 350 yards to the far side of a canal bridge.

78 Short Walks Made Easy

**Above**: fallow deer
**Top right**: painted lady
**Middle right**: red admiral
**Far right**: mallards
**Right**: hedge bindweed

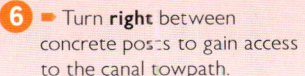

☆ Bridgewater Canal

Oldfield Brow

4 miles   4½ miles   5 miles

Trans Pennine Trail car park

**6** ▸ Turn **right** between concrete posts to gain access to the canal towpath.
▸ Keep **forward**, walking away from the bridge, beside the Bridgewater Canal for 1 mile to white railings just after the next bridge.

**7** ▸ At the railings, turn **left** on a path that cuts through to Seamons Road. Turn **right** along the road back to the car park

Walk 10 Dunham Massey 79

## Publishing information

© Crown copyright 2025.
All rights reserved.

Ordnance Survey, OS, and the OS logos are registered trademarks, and OS Short Walks Made Easy is a trademark of Ordnance Survey Ltd.

© Crown copyright and database rights (2025) Ordnance Survey.

ISBN 978 0 319092 96 5
1st edition published by Ordnance Survey 2025.

ordnancesurvey.co.uk

While every care has been taken to ensure the accuracy of the route directions, the publishers cannot accept responsibility for errors or omissions, or for changes in details given. The countryside is not static: hedges and fences can be removed, stiles can be replaced by gates, field boundaries can alter, footpaths can be rerouted and changes in ownership can result in the closure or diversion of some concessionary paths. Also, paths that are easy and pleasant for walking in fine conditions may become slippery, muddy and difficult in wet weather.

If you find an inaccuracy in either the text or maps, please contact Ordnance Survey at os.uk/contact.

All rights reserved. No part of this publication may be reproduced, transmitted in any form or by any means, or stored in a retrieval system without either the prior written permission of the publisher, or in the case of reprographic reproduction a licence issued in accordance with the terms and licences issued by the CLA Ltd.

A catalogue record for this book is available from the British Library.

## Milestone Publishing credits

**Author:** John Gillham

**Series editor:** Kevin Freeborn

**Maps:** Cosmographics

**Design and Production:** Patrick Dawson, Milestone Publishing

Printed in India by Replika Press Pvt. Ltd

## Photography credits

**Front cover** ©John Gillham. **Back cover** cornfield/Shutterstock.com.

All photographs supplied by the author ©John Gillham except page 6 Samantha Meekin (Ordnance Survey); page 19 Fiona Baltrop; page 33 Felicity Martin. The following images were supplied by **Alamy Stock Photos**: page 45 Barbara Cook; 51 Chronicle; 57 Steve Robinson. The following images were supplied by **Shutterstock.com**: page 1 Gail Kelsall; 17 Joe Dunckley; 24 Erni; 33 Sandra Standbrid. The following images were supplied via **Wikimedia Commons under CC BY 2.0** <https:// creative commons.org/licenses/by/2.0>: page 25 Jacob Spinks; 25 Oliver Dixon; 26 Dom Crossley; 33 Mike Pennington; 38 David Dixon; 38 Mick Lobb; 38 gilgit2; 40 Steve F; 44 Paul Anderson; 47 Ian Greig; 47 David Lally; 53 David Wright; 58 Penny Mayes; 59 Kenneth Allen; 59 Paco Gómez; 59 Evelyn Simak; 59 Neil Theasby; 59 David Dixon; 67 Cj Hughson; 73 Bikeboy; 73 Mike Pennington; 77 David Dixon; 78 Sylvia Duckworth; 79 Jeff Buck; 79 Philip Halling. The following images were supplied via **Wikimedia Commons under CC BY 2.50** <https:// creative commons.org/licenses/by/2.5>: 53 Aleph; 67, 79 Richard Bartz; Andreas Trepte. The following images were supplied via **Wikimedia Commons under CC BY 3.0** <https:// creative commons.org/licenses/by/3.0>: page 33, 67 Quartl; 41 Ken Billington; 53 Mathias Krumbholz; 64 Clem Rutter; 73 Aiwok. The following images were supplied via **Wikimedia Commons under CC BY 4.0** <https:// creative commons.org/licenses/by/4.0>: 39, 47 Charles J. Sharp; 39 Mildeep; 40 Christoph Müller; 41 Alexis Lours; 41 Francis C. Franklin; 46 kmtextor; 67 T. Kebert; 72 Zeynel Cebeci; 79 Syrio. The following images were supplied under **Public domain, via Wikimedia Commons**: page 21 W.H.Holl engraving; 49 ILN Staff, The London Illustrated News.